DETERMINATION + CORE VALUES

$UCCE$$

A Business-Building Guidebook for New Wellness Entrepreneurs

TERRANCE BONNER, CEO, LMT, LE

Determination + CORE Values = Success
A Business-Building Guide for New Wellness Entrepreneurs

First published by Powerful Potential & Purpose Publishing 2020

Copyright © 2020 by Powerful Potential & Purpose Publishing

First printing, December 2020

Cover art, graphics and book design by Candy Lyn Thomen
Photos courtesy of Pixabay and Pexels

ISBN: 978-1-7349655-8-2

Published in USA

www.PPP-Publishing.com
Hickory, NC - USA

DEDICATION

To my mom, who taught me so much in life.
The greatest advice, *"Always get what you want and never settle."*
In 2004 she told me this and it has always remained with me.

Thank you, Mom.

CONTENTS

CONTENTS

Congratulations!

I would like to welcome and congratulate you on taking the first step to learn about the core foundations that will help you succeed as a business owner.

Whether you are thinking about opening a business or perhaps you already are an aspiring owner; no matter where you may be on your path, this book will help you along the journey of being an entrepreneur.

You know this book is exactly right for you if:

- ✓ You are an aspiring business owner and scared to take that leap of faith

- ✓ You are a new business owner struggling because everything is not adding up

- ✓ You are looking to be an expert in your field

- ✓ You do not know how to make a profit and calculate your cost per service

- ✓ You are not paying yourself like you should be

- ✓ You need marketing and promotion support and ideas

- ✓ You are confused about the banking options, how to find an accountant or create a business plan

- ✓ You seek inspiration to understand why your core values are your driving force to success and much more

INTRODUCTION

Photo ©Brandon Morgan

GOD'S PLAN FOR ME

I believe God had a plan for me that was predestined. You see, even at 4 years old, growing up in Mississippi, I knew. A speeding train could have killed my mom and me, but I am here to share my success story. This was just a taste of what God can do. I hope to inspire you.

We headed early one morning to the babysitter's house to drop me off for the day. As usual, Mom was running late. We were racing down the road, Mom was speeding and in a hurry to get to work.

"Oh NO, not today!" she yelled.

I watched her speed up, defying the odds to beat the train. I still remember the determination on her face while I was playing with my toy in the rear seat. A horrid screeching sound was coming from her tires as she jammed on the brakes, rapidly turning the steering wheel to avoid the oncoming train.

"Are you okay, baby?" she asked, breathing heavily with a terrified look on her face.

"Yes, Mama, I'm okay," as I looked back over my shoulder noticing the dust had cleared. Our car was facing the wrong direction as the high-speed train continued down the tracks. We almost got hit! Surely there is a reason I am here to tell this story now.

Determination would become my driving force.

When we finally arrived at Ms. Rosie's house the cartoons quickly distracted me from feeling shook up. Ms. Rosie was my favorite sitter, so smart, and she always knew how to settle me down. She loved to cook too. I will always remember her sweet, loving and kind personality. At the delicate age of four, I was already attuned to the caring nature of people. This would go with me through life.

Ms. Rosie worked hard taking care of a lot of children over the years. It became more challenging as she got older and Mom knew she would eventually have to find a new sitter for me. That did not make me a happy camper at all. I was so comfortable in her loving environment; I did not want to go anywhere else. There is something to be said for comfortable environments and feeling safe.

I felt like a big man at five, and the time had come for a new sitter. Honestly, I did not feel that same connection with her. The vibe was all wrong, and I didn't sense the same love. It's quite interesting as I reminisce how I was sensing all this at such a young age and would be the gift I take forward in my career.

When we took our naps on the hard floor or uncomfortable couch, I would miss Ms. Rosie and her love. Her house had three bedrooms, a gigantic living room to play, dining room and the kitchen which all felt like home. Having a place to feel comfortable was my happy place.

I noticed my new sitter was lazy, sleeping a lot on the job too. You probably can see how my work ethics were already astute. I made a plan in my head to escape one day while she was sleeping. Every step was in my head and which turn I had to take. Yep, I had a plan, and it was going to work. I just knew it.

The day came. Sure, I was a little nervous as I slowly unlocked the door and began my journey from one end of the south side of town to the other. There it was, Ms. Rosie's house. I firmly knocked on her door and with a puzzled look on her face, she opened the door to let me in. Ah, I was home. Just like old times, my baby sitter proceeding to the kitchen to make me a little breakfast. Then for lunch she would cook up my favorite chicken and dumplings.

Later that day, the "knock, knock" on the door came from my mom.
"Is Terrance here?"

"Why yes, he's in the back watching TV," Ms. Rosie replied.

I could hear footsteps getting louder and closer and my eyes getting wider when suddenly Mom screamed "My baby!" She gave me the biggest hug. I guess I scared her a little on that day. I had decided to do something, and I did it, but I failed to realize how Mom might feel.

Looking back, this was a pivotal moment in my life. I realize this small town African-American boy can put his mind to anything that may seem impossible and no matter how far off it seems, I CAN make it happen. The spirit God put in this little body was a force to be reckoned with, I'd say. I felt like my favorite superhero, Batman, who always had a dedication to a purpose and went directly to the heart of the matter.

> *"It's not who I am underneath,*
> *but what I do that defines me."*
>
> *Bruce Wayne/Batman*

Photo ©Brandon Morgan

I truly believe God knew I was predestined to help others in life. It was a miracle we missed that train. Many miracles happened in life, as if I was being watched over all the time. Even the years I spent in the Baptist church, as the minister of music directing the choir, I realize now everything that happened was preparing me for Life and all the obstacles, trials and accomplishments I would face. That purpose and plan is still being unraveled till this very day.

LEARNING OBJECTIVES

After applying the information in this guide, you will know:

- How to determine your core key values to keep you going
- How to set up your business step by step
- How to successfully write a business plan
- Key things to determine when searching for an accountant
- Knowing the difference between banks and choosing the right one for you
- Learn how to determine your cost of services and what your profit margin will be
- Marketing and promotion so you can get published in the places to gain visibility for your business success

LEARNING OUTCOMES

You will be able to:

- Determine what is your core value
- Demonstrate a simple business plan
- Determine your cost per service
- Show how to create a business card and brochure
- Show how to write a press release
- Determine all the right marketing strategies for success
- Determine where to start with this step-by-step approach

SECTION ONE

ARE YOU READY TO BE AN ENTREPRENEUR?

This section will introduce you to the key factors which will help determine if you are ready to be an entrepreneur. Things such as core values, personal strengths and the role models in your life will help you succeed.

CHAPTER ONE

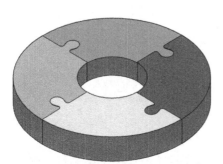

CORE VALUES

I have come to learn how important core values helped me achieve my goals. I have included this because they are the fundamental beliefs of a person or organization. When I viewed other similar books, this component seemed to be missing. I realized this was my unique offering to my audience. The piece that held it all together through every trial and tribulation.

When I shared my story, I realized these guiding principles dictated my behavior and outcome. I didn't even realize it at first.

Core values guide companies to determine if they are fulfilling their goals by creating an unwavering commitment .

These are some examples of the negative core values we may identify in our life. I want to support you in finding your positive ones to achieve.

- A belief the world is a fundamentally a hard place and that only the strong survive
- A belief people are powerless to change personal situations
- A belief you don't deserve good things or relationships in life
- A belief you or other people are unloving or non-deserving
- A belief life is meaningless

MY OWN CORE VALUES

FAITH

As I entered my career as a massage therapist and esthetician, my goal was to become my own boss by owning my business. I honestly did not realize what it all entailed or how to begin. As I wrote everything down I needed, such as equipment and the vision of my space, I would come to realize something later on, much later actually. The journey I took had me take a leap of faith. I knew with the preparation I had done I would be ready. Faith is my number one core value, actually my driving force. Remember, at four in my story, I depended on faith, even to get me to Ms. Rosie's house. Faith, the size of a mustard seed, is all I needed to get through. I am still here to share my story and provide inspiration. Do you have faith? Faith for me forced me to step out of my comfort zone. I would hear "no" after "no" not completely understanding the message. My 5-year goal was built upon Faith. God had plans that were not mine. Along the way however, God saw fit for me to open in the divine timing of four years.

DETERMINATION

Every "*No*" pushed me harder to my destination. Determination is another core value, perhaps my second strongest. It pushed me through everything and made me a better person. Even writing this book took more than I ever imagined. Without determination and faith, you would not be reading this now.

I was on cloud nine when I received my dual licensing. It was like no one and nothing could bring me down. I was so enthusiastic and proud to hold those two licenses. All I ever wanted to do was help others have a good sense about themselves, live healthier and bring a better outlook to them through massage and esthetics.

The No's poured out and doorways closed. How could this be happening when I knew this was my purpose? I was more determined actually to prove something to myself. Maybe God was testing me? I had doubt, fears, and people who were against me for whatever reason. Yet I knew I was gifted and it would not go to waste.

When you have a burning desire and know it is right for you, you must keep going. I will not lie and say that this shit did not hurt. It went deep and hurt badly, even when I had conversations with people close to me. I was not making any money at the time. I heard, "You should get a regular 'real' job. At least you will know you will have a steady paycheck coming in". I felt defeated.

My faith was strong and no matter how many times there were naysayers, I believed at my core and with my determination I could prove to myself, I can do this. Let nothing cloud your judgment when you believe this deeply that you have a purpose.

DEDICATION

Finding your purpose may be easy for some and others it could take a lifetime. It's also more than a job, a career. It's much deeper. It's that driving force that is unstoppable. It's the knowing you are meant for something more, even when you can't put your finger on it.

It took time; it did not show up or manifest quickly. I remember listening to recruiters in high school and when they mentioned massage therapy, something resonated deep within me. It stood out like a sore thumb. My family had no clue what it meant and encouraged me to pursue working with computers. I listened and went into animation and design. Although I hated it, it wasn't the end of the world. Yep, I quit. Doesn't sound much like determination, does it? However, I had dedication to pursue something I knew was in my heart and soul and I would not stop.

I moved back to Mississippi to pursue my passion in massage therapy. Hurricane Katrina landed, and the school had shut down. I found another and fell it love with it during the tour. Everything seemed 'right' about it. I was accepted and enrolled that day. Many things were challenging because of the hurricane, and it was impossible for me to find an affordable place to live.

More road blocks. Was this meant for me? Why? I had to tell the school I could not afford to do it now. I was so down in the dumps. The calling was so passionate, I knew it would dedicate me to this purpose and one day I would hold that license as a massage therapist.

I am now dedicated to provide comfort to my clients and an environment for all that come through the doors of my wellness spa to gain a sense of being welcomed and find their own healing path.

COMPASSION

Two years went by and the thought of attending massage school never left my mind. I was feeling really down one day when a friend at KFC, where I worked, noticed and asked me what was wrong. "I am tired of working here and ready to move on," I replied to her. When I heard her say "Awe, you will be here the rest of your life and you're not going anywhere" I knew in that moment "hell no" that is not my path even though I had 10 years of employment and benefits. Maybe she was joking, I'm not sure, but those words lit a fire under me like no other.

Yes, you guessed it! I found a school nearby, researched it and was determined to go no matter what my parents would say. No ifs, ands or buts! I was persistent. They required me to take an entrance exam, which made me a tad bit nervous, however, I proceeded. When he interviewed me with questions, I realized something deeper. It was then he said, "I can hear compassion in your voice and that you really want to help others." Yes, that was it! Compassion kept me pursuing this profession. Sometimes we don't identify our own core values, but someone may help us along the way to navigate our course to help others. I have always had compassion and in my opinion, it is crucial for my business. Since I was 6 years old, I always wanted to help others and now, finally, I was in my happy place.

I thought about all the years my mom pushed me. While she was hard on me, both my parents had work ethics I am proud of. It's my legacy as well. Even though back in those days I would ask her if she 'had it out for me,' as she was my boss at KFC too. I was proud of Mom when she won an award and I hope she is proud of me now. I have a sense of her sometimes watching over me. *Yes Mom, I understand you prepared me for all of this, no doubt.* I wish I could tell her in person how thankful I am today.

Photo by @bmorgansphotography

IDENTIFYING YOUR POSITIVE CORE VALUES

Ask yourself the following questions and use the workbook pages to establish what your four cornerstone values are and the most powerful one that runs deep within your core for a total of five. Four corner stones and one central driving force. If you don't know them all, you will see them unfold as you build your business and evaluate your personal life and relationships.

1. *What brings you the most joy in life?*
2. *What provides meaning to your life?*
3. *What is your guiding principle to do well in life?*
4. *What would you want to achieve?*
5. *What is the one thing that seems to keep you going?*
6. *Do you have firm beliefs?*
7. *What are the central beliefs that guide your actions?*

It's also important to remember individuals don't necessarily choose their core values. Many people have these values instilled in them by their parents and the surrounding community. You may already live by strong core values without realizing it.

In considering this business guide book, I wanted to bring something I don't see everywhere. It felt that the insights of your core values are a key to determining your success.

1. What brings you the most joy in life?

2. What provides meaning to your life?

3. What is your guiding principle to do well in life?

4. What would you want to achieve?

5. What is the one thing that seems to keep you going?

6. Do you have firm beliefs? List what they are:

7. What are the central beliefs that guide your actions?

To help you get started, here are some examples of core values from which you may wish to choose:

❏ Dependability
❏ Reliability
❏ Loyalty
❏ Commitment
❏ Open-mindedness
❏ Consistency
❏ Honesty
❏ Faith
❏ Compassion
❏ Motivation

❏ Determination
❏ Dedication
❏ Creativity
❏ Optimism
❏ Motivation
❏ Adventurous
❏ Innovation
❏ Passionate
❏ Courageous
❏ Perseverance

Write down your personal core values:

Notes, Thoughts and Ideas:

COMPANY CORE VALUES

These are the guiding principles that help to define how the corporation should behave in business. They have a mission to serve the community. Core values are usually expressed in the corporation's mission statement.

Some examples of core values for a company include:

- A commitment to sustainability and to acting in an environmentally friendly way.
- A commitment to innovation and excellence.
- A commitment to doing good for the whole.
- A commitment to caring for others.

What are the Core Values you would want for your business:

CHAPTER TWO

ENTREPRENEUR

What determines a successful entrepreneur?

"I'm convinced that about half of what separates successful entrepreneurs from the non-successful ones is pure perseverance."

- Steve Jobs

An entrepreneur, to me, is a visionary. A person who can see the full picture, not just the edges on the frame. Someone who is not afraid when times get hard and they keep going. They would never quit. Becoming an entrepreneur successfully, is difficult but is extremely rewarding.

I was a visionary. In 2010 we did a project in massage school and I still have it. I designed a spa. While I encountered negativity, let downs and disappointment, nothing stopped my vision from coming to fruition.

ROLE MODELS

Did you have a role model growing up or someone you admired? I had
Batman, my mom, and Ms. Rosie. Three role models that had influence over
me in positive ways.

Who are your role models?

What characteristics do they portray that you admire?

Do you have these traits? List your top three:

1.

2.

3.

If you don't have these traits, what do you need to do to acquire them?

If you could ask any famous person in the world a question about how they became successful, who would it be, why and what question would you ask them?

Person's Name:

Why would you ask this person?

What question would you ask them:

Now ask yourself the same question. How would you respond?

Let's look at a few famous people and see if you can identify their **CORE VALUES**, their *"what brought them success."*

BENJAMIN FRANKLIN

Benjamin was innovative and created some wacky experiments. He was always up to something. They credit Franklin for creating the lightning rod, bifocals and more, even though he had many flops. Like many famous people, he wore a thousand hats. He was a scientist, politician, inventor, author, and savvy businessman to name a few.

Can you identify with Benjamin Franklin? Why?

HANS CHRISTIAN ANDERSEN

Hans had fierce determination and was a self-starter. He grew up poor in Copenhagen and at the age of fourteen, a fortune teller told him he would suffer early in life and one day would be famous.

Anderson was teased and harassed in school. One day the director at Royal Danish Theater saw something special in him and took him under his wing.

What do you relate to?

MADAM C.J. WALKER

They regarded this amazing woman as the first black self-made American millionaire. She was born in 1867 on a Louisiana plantation. She was a visionary and created a solution to a problem no one else was interested in solving. She started her own line of beauty and hair products specifically designed for black women. She embodies the entrepreneurial spirit and fought tooth and nail to step up that ladder.

What do you admire about Madam Walker?

You may wonder why I'm sharing this information and asking you these questions. It's important because the people that influence your life are the ones that can bring you down or raise you up to succeed.

Have you ever heard the phrase, *"You're the average of the five people you spend the most time with,"* spoken by the very successful motivational speaker, Jim Rohn?

TIME FOR SOME SELF EVALUATION:

What key components of an Entrepreneur do you identify within yourself?

- ❏ Passion
- ❏ Vision
- ❏ Perseverance
- ❏ Good Listener
- ❏ Excellent communicator
- ❏ Proactive

- ❏ Adaptability
- ❏ Self confidence
- ❏ Patience
- ❏ Risk Taker
- ❏ Responsible

Why do you want to be an entrepreneur? List ALL of your reasons, even if they don't feel like they apply:

Do you identify with a product or service?

What are your reasons? (list as many as you want)

1.

2.

3.

4.

5.

6.

Healthy habits of a successful entrepreneur - Which ones do you have?

❏ Create a routine

❏ Get up earlier than usual

❏ Meditate and/or pray

❏ Workout frequently

❏ Time block your day to stay on course

❏ Do your most challenging tasks first

❏ Schedule income-producing activities

❏ Track your progress

❏ Eat well

❏ Take trainings to better yourself

❏ Enjoy quality time with family and friends

Where are your strengths?

Where do you need to develop yourself more?

1.

2.

3.

4.

Ask yourself *"are you ready?"*

❑ **Yes!**   ❑ **No**   ❑ **Almost**   ✔

If you answered **Yes!** or **Almost**, then you are ready to get started. If you said **No**, take a shot at it. It may surprise you.

There will never be the 'right' time to begin your business. However, you can look at what is holding you back.

Make a list:

1.

2.

3.

4.

5.

Do you have what it takes to be an entrepreneur?

Circle the ones that apply to you:

Smart Risk-Taker

Detailed Oriented

Continuously Seeking Improvement

Impeccable Communication Skills

Strategic Thought Processor

Determination

SECTION TWO

IDEA - PLAN - ACTION

This section will lead you through the process of first dreaming about then developing the IDEA for your business, the PLAN for what to do and how to get it started, and the ACTION steps necessary to get it off the ground and running.

CHAPTER THREE

YOUR BUSINESS DREAM / IDEA

Dreaming is fun! It is from our dreams that ideas begin to take shape and form. Writing down your dreams can help you learn a lot about yourself and what you truly want in the process. No dream is too big or too small. Whatever you want is just right!

What is your passion and/or niche?

What is your dream of being a business owner or entrepreneur?

What kind of business do you want to open?

How long do you expect it will take to open?

Will you have employees? How many?

"How much do I need to start my business?"

This is the most common question I receive.
The answer depends on the type of business you desire.
Are you a massage therapist, baker, graphic designer,
boutique owner, production company, free-lancer, make-
up artist, stylist, cosmetologist, nail tech, esthetician, etc.?

This guidebook will provide the steps and valuable
information you can apply to most businesses.

A little advice, invest in yourself and not the opinions of others. It is sad but
true, not everyone is your advocate. People may make promises to support
your business and never actually use your service. It does not mean everyone
will be an investor in your business or your future, but the ones who are meant
to be, will be. Remain positive and focused on your dream.

So, years went by and I said the heck with it I am going to do it. I became a
client of a local business and my intentions were to talk to the owners once
they became familiar with me; I was not sure if they knew who I was or not, to
mention how I would love to set up some type of referral between our
businesses. Eventually, after running into each other at different events, after I
became a client, the owner began encouraging me to keep doing what I was
doing because I was receiving a lot of high praise. That alone to me was
amazing. Eventually the owner became a client of mine as well. After the one
visit I received a phone call from their business requesting business cards and
brochures so they could refer their clients to me. In my head I was thinking,
"This is what I wanted, and I did not have to say it." My work did the speaking
for me.

With those extra referrals, it boosted my sales by 30%. That is an extra 30% I
did not spend a penny on to make. I accomplished the goal and intention. It
all came from me thinking outside the box. You must do the work to get the
results you want. You can not expect to make $100,000 and sleep in 3-4 days a
week and leave early. You must have determination and commitment to be
successful. It helps to have creative business thinking.

HOW MUCH WILL I NEED TO OPEN MY BUSINESS?

This question is asked a lot, and that depends on how big your business is? What will you need to open?

SMALL BUSINESS

The service is minimal, you maybe only need a massage table, lotion or cream and a filing cabinet. No products, no inventory, just you and your few things.

Total cost= $1,500

PLUS operating expenses for 3-6 months to help sustain you. You will not make a profit at first, but your operating expenses will help you through that period.

FULL-SERVICE BUSINESS

This is a full service, product and inventory-based business. You would need full equipment for 3-4 rooms, office furniture, products, full inventory, and staff.

Total Cost = $6,000-$10,000

PLUS operating expenses for 6-12 months to help sustain you. Again, you will not make a profit at first, but your operating expenses will help you through that period.

With both models, you will need to calculate your total cost of equipment and supplies needed to open.

Remember, starting small is better than not starting at all.

How much do you have to invest?

What can you do to start your business with little to no investment?

How can I grow my business even more?

These are significant questions to answer and provide you an honest
projection and assessment for a starting point in your business.

HOW SOON CAN I OPEN?

My first question would be, *"Do you already have a clientele?"*

I would suggest having a clientele before opening to help sustain you. The only way any business stays open is by having repeat clients.

Think about your favorite store and how much you **LOVE** shopping there. With this in mind, answer the following questions:

Why do you shop at this store?

What do you LOVE about this particular store or establishment?

Where will you find your clientele and how will you get them in your doorway? (more on this later)

Do not rush. I suggest giving yourself three to six months to open. Factor in necessary things like your business license, rent or mortgage payment, lights, deposits if needed, equipment, privilege license and so on. You want to give yourself time to make sure once your clients come in, they experience greatness in your new business and come back. Follow my steps and it will prepare you for success.

TARGET AUDIENCE

Who would be the target audience for your business? The people who want your service or product?

What is the age and income bracket of your target audience?

TIME TO DO YOUR MARKET RESEARCH

Are there similar businesses in your region?

Where are they located?

What exactly do they offer? List both services and products:

What are their prices?

What days of the week are they open? What are their hours?

Are they selling online as well?

How large is the facility? What size do you want?

What did you like? From what you saw, what do you never want to do?

**Jot down all the things you find out
about two similar types of businesses.**

Notes, Thoughts and Ideas:

CHAPTER FOUR

PLAN

Set Realistic Goals and Expectations

Most people will fail within one year and many will close shop within three years because they were naïve about expectations. They also did not calculate their finances correctly and what they need in reserve for expenses.

> *"The people that want to step into their greatness are hungry."*
> *— Les Brown*

Immediate Goal: within 1 day to 30 days

Short Term Goal: Goals 1 month up to 9 months, less than 1 year

Long term Goals: 1 year, 5 years, 10 years.

On the following worksheet, jot down your goals. List 2 Immediate, **2 Short Term** and **2 Long Term goals.**

For example:

I will begin to research locations this month and create my dream board no later than (date) _____

I desire to open _____
on or about (date). _____

My location will be _____
and my market will be _____

_____

I have $ _____ *to begin my business*
and need $ _____ *for supplies, etc.*
I also have $ _____ *for* _____ *months of reserve.*

It is my goal to have _____ *amount of customers daily/weekly.*
I will hire _____ *employees.*

Keep adding what your goals are to the worksheet. You have to know what you want.

All of this information becomes your basic business plan.

List Two IMMEDIATE GOALS (1 day – 30 days)

List Two SHORT TERM GOALS (1 month – 9 months)

List Three LONG TERM GOALS (1 year, 5 year, 10 year)

THINK OUTSIDE THE BOX:

To think outside the box means to stretch yourself into an uncomfortable space, try new things, and be one step ahead of your game. Think in the terms of what makes you '*unique*' and how will it intrigue your community and global market if you sell online.

> *"If you build a great experience, customers will tell each other about it. Word of mouth is very powerful."*
> ~ Jeff Bezos (one of the wealthiest men in the world)

MY EXPERIENCE: When people told me it's already been done or there is a similar business nearby, I worked harder to create a unique concept and experience. No one will work harder than you in your own business! I know this personally. You are birthing your vision ~ push through it! Nurture it and it will grow.

Write down 3 things that scare you?

1.

2.

3.

Write down 3 things you would love to do with your business, but you don't know how.

1.

2.

3.

Write down 3 resources or people that may provide the insight(s) you need to make your dream come true.

1.

2.

3.

Get a business coach! A business coach not only helps you outline your vision, they provide the support and inspiration to bring out your potential. They can see things you may miss. The value of a coach is worth every cent if you find one more successful than you who has done what you desire.

VISION & MISSION

Creating your vision and mission statement

What is a vision statement?

A vision statement is the anchor point of any strategic plan. It outlines what your organization would like to aspire to and the guiding beacon to all within your organization. It determines the intended direction of your company. A good statement should be concise and specific to your business.

When I think of famous visionaries, Jeff Bezos, Oprah and Michael Jackson come to mind. They knew what it was they wanted, they had help, and they took their first step to flourish, but not overnight.

> *"The greatest education in the world is watching the masters at work."*
> –Michael Jackson

What is a mission statement?

A mission summarizes the core purpose of your business organization. It includes what you focus on and aim for your customers. It usually briefly describes what the organization does and its key objectives. This is your roadmap for the company's vision statement.

What's the difference between the two?

In short: The *mission* is the WHAT and HOW and the *vision* is the WHY.

I will include a more detailed business plan later in the guidebook if you need one for a financial institution for a loan approval.

This is a blueprint, like a map to get you started.

Create a vision statement that is so clear nothing will stop you!

Some companies combine both statements into one clearly defined reason for existing that may unite the efforts of everyone involved.

Example of my vision:

I wanted a full-service salon and spa. One place for my clients to get everything they desired accomplished in one space.

Create a mission statement

Thoughts - Notes - Questions

BASIC BUSINESS PLAN – Short Plan

I will include a more detailed business plan later in the guidebook if you need one for a financial institution for a loan approval.

This is a blueprint, like a map to get you started.

Name of business:

Location:

Estimated opening date:

What will you sell or offer:

Who needs it:

What other services or providers are offering similar products and services to yours?

How will your business fit into the local market?

What is your vision?

What is your mission statement?

Describe your company in detail:

A company description outlines all the vital details about your company, including what you hope to accomplish. It also includes your vision and the direction of company growth and potential partners.

Once you complete this basic plan, get feedback from a trusted source. *Ex., lawyer, accountant, successful business owner. Someone in the know.*

A great resource for assistance could be found in local community organizations with retired entrepreneurs. Ask your chamber of commerce for referrals to these networking resources.

ESTIMATED START-UP EXPENSES

ESTIMATED COST – Depending on your region and what you decide on for equipment, décor and rental fees, these amounts will vary.

Opening Business Checking Account	$100
Internet Installation/Activation	$199
Equipment	$2,000 - $5000
First & Last Month's Rent/Security Deposit	$3,000
Business Cards	$125
Service Menu/Brochure	$200
Company Logo	$200-$600+
Website	$500
Décor	$300 and up
Office Supplies	$550
Scheduling System	$199
Alarm System	$200
Phone Service/Installation	$199
Total Approximately	**$7770 and up**

Estimated Annual Expenses

Write in your own cost

Property Insurance	$500
Business License & Building Permit	$150
Legal & Accounting Fee	$500
Liability Insurance	$199
Professional Association Membership	$200
Chamber of Commerce Member Fee	$250
*Education (workshops, seminars, classes)	$500

Estimated Monthly Expenses

Rent	$1,500
Utilities	$175
Phone Service	$75
Internet Service	$125
Bank Fees	$40
Supplies	$65
Marketing	$150
Travel Expenses	$75
Inventory	$250
Staff Salary	TBD
Your Salary	$2,000
Website Maintenance	$30
Alarm System	$35

Add anything else you can think of depending on your personal needs:

FUNDING YOUR PROJECT

Most people save money to generate what they will need for costs, taxes, rent and six months of savings for salary or unexpected expenses.

How will you fund your business project?

- ❏ Savings
- ❏ Loan
- ❏ Family Gift
- ❏ Fund raiser
- ❏ Other _____

How much do you have saved currently?

How long will it take you to save the start up costs?

IDEAL CLIENT

Let's identify your ideal client—the more specific you are, the better you will align with your '*ideal*' client.

Keep in mind this is the "ideal" and you will have other clients, but ask yourself ***WHO DO YOU WANT TO ATTRACT.***

Gender:

Median age:

Occupation(s):

Median salary:

Where do they hang out? Coffee shops? Book stores? etc.

Are they a health coach, if you are in the wellness field?

Write down all the characteristics of your ideal client:

Write down their needs, also known as pain points. Why do they need YOU and your services or product?

Ex. *They are in pain and need a massage; They desire their skin to be healthier*
They are stressed and need to relax

LOCATION, LOCATION, LOCATION

Think for a moment of how a restaurant positions their business.

> **Where is the closest facility similar to yours?**

Determine a region you desire that would best suit your ***ideal client.***
Be open to options and ideas you may not have considered. Make an
appointment to visit the properties and take a list of all the things you want to
have in your space. Some places may require renovations.

> **What size would be ideal for you? 1200 sq. feet to start? Less? More?**

Is it a high traffic area? Visible and easy to find?

What business surrounding the location may be excellent referral sources?

FACILITY VISION BOARD

It's fun to design and outline your space. Create a sample idea of what you desire on the worksheet to the right.

Reception area
Seating area
How many rooms for treatments? _____
Retail space
Gathering space for meditation, classes or lectures

Next, what is the ideal size of each room?
8x 10 , 9 x 12, _____ x _____

Lighting
Carpeting or tile
Sink
Closet
Shelves

I would suggest when you visit other facilities to jot ideas down and take photos.

Create a diagram of your dream space:

OPERATION HOURS

What days of the week do you want to be open for business?

What are your ideal hours?

Will you have employees? If yes, how many?

Will you have a receptionist or use answering service?

Sub contractors or employees?

What are the benefits and obligations of both? Review this with your accountant

YOUR DREAM BUSINESS BOARD

Create a vision/dream board. Get a large poster board. Cut out pictures and words that represent everything you desire for your business.

- *Include a picture of yourself in the center*
- *Be specific about financial goals*
- *Include pictures that may look like your facility*
- *Include customer pictures that would want your service*
- *Have fun creating*

Every action step you take brings you one step closer.

ESTABLISH YOUR TEAM

Establishing the right team to carry out your vision is extremely important for success. Know your own strengths and weaknesses and those of the people you hire.

- Align people where they will be best suited
- Don't expect someone to do things they are not capable of unless they are willing to learn
- Hire people who are motivated.
- Motivation is different for each individual. Do they have similar interest and goals?
- Are they team players in order to help you obtain your goals?
- How will you motivate and compensate them when goals are met?
- Listen to their ideas.
- What does their journey look include?

"To accomplish great things, we must not only act but also dream; not only plan but also believe."
~ Anatole France

CHAPTER FIVE

ACTION

"Action is the foundational key to all success. "

~ Pablo Picasso

Use the worksheet at the right to make your plan of action. Begin with the simple things and start dreaming. Review the vision boards you recently created in Chapter 5. If you haven't created yours yet, I strongly recommend you do so before proceeding with this section.

❏ *What is the first thing you must do?*

❏ *Who will help you?*

❏ *Where will you locate your business?*

❏ *What are your basic startup costs involved?*

❏ *Do you have an accountant?*

❏ *Do you know if you want to be a solopreneur or partner?*

❏ *Will you have a sole proprietorship, LLC or Corporation?*

❏ *Do you have an idea of your business name? Experiment with it.*

❏ *Do you know how to set up a business checking account?*

What is the first thing you must do? Refer to your Immediate Goals on page 57

Who will help you?

Where will you locate your business? Refer to your Basic Business Plan on page 66

Do you have an idea of your business name? Experiment with it.

What are your basic startup costs involved? Refer to Startup Costs on page 70

Do you know how to set up a business checking account?
Refer to Business Banking starting on page 97

Do you have an accountant? Refer to Choosing the Right Account on page 100

Do you know if you want to be a solopreneur or partner?

Will you have a sole proprietorship, LLC or Corporation?
Refer to Business Entity Types starting on page 87

WHICH TYPE OF BUSINESS ENTITY IS RIGHT FOR YOU?

When starting your business, one of the first things you want to do is choose the structure of your company—in other words, choose a business entity type.

In simplest terms, a business entity is created by an individual or individuals to conduct business. A business's entity type dictates the structure of that business.

Sole Proprietorship

An unincorporated business owned and run by one individual with no distinction between the business and you, the owner.

PROS OF SOLE PROPRIETORSHIP

- **The owner enjoys all the profits of the business:** since it is owned by a single person; he enjoys all the profits that the business accrues.

- **Little to no startup cost**

- **Easy to Manage:** As a single business owner, it easy to manage your business since there is no bureaucracy that you must follow when making decisions.

- **Flexibility:** This applies in terms of changing the commodities you sell. You can change them anytime you feel like as long as it is a general sole proprietorship with freedom to sell any product.

- No state filing requirements (depending on your state).

CONS OF SOLE PROPRIETORSHIP

- **The owner incurs all the losses:** In case of losses, the sole proprietor bares all the burden solely.

- **Unlimited liability:** This means that in case the business runs bankrupt, the assets of the business owner will be sold to clear off the debts.

- The business owner pays personal income taxes on the business' net profits.

- Less Professional

- Difficult to raise capital

General Partnership

A partnership is a business entity owned and operated by two or more individuals. The partners contribute money to raise the required capital to start the business. All of them are responsible for how the business operates and take part in decision-making. The partners might allocate each of them a unique role to enhance the efficiency and performance of the entity. If you would like to start a general partnership, have a look at the pros and cons.

PROS OF GENERAL PARTNERSHIP

- **Easy to Start:** Forming a general partnership usually takes a short time since it does not involve long legal procedures.

- **Requires less capital:** The amount required to start off a partnership is not equal to the amount you need to start a company. They share the amount of profits according to the ratio of capital contribution of each partner. The higher the capital you contributed, the more the profits you enjoy.

- **Consultation:** The good thing with partnerships is that before arriving at a final decision, there is always consultation between the partners. This leads to better decisions that improve the business.

- **Quick Decision Making:** A partnership owned and operated by two people is easy to make decisions that can enhance the performance of the business. You need not call a meeting to discuss arising issues, just a phone call is enough.

CONS OF GENERAL PARTNERSHIP

- **Unlimited liability:** General partnerships means that all the partners have unlimited liability. In case of business debts that the business cannot pay, the personal assets of the partners are at risk of getting sold to clear off the debt.

- **Internal Wrangles:** Sometimes many partnerships fail because of internal conflicts or personal interests of a certain partner. The partners have a burden of paying personal income taxes on the net profits of the business.

- **Less independence**

- **Must split profits**

Limited Liability Partnership (LLP)

A limited type of partnership is whereby all the individuals have limited liability unlike general partnerships where all partners have unlimited liability. A partnership operates as a limited type only after the partners apply for registration, accountants, or doctors.

However, nowadays even common businesses may apply for registration for as long as the partnership has partners that run and operate the business and partners who act as investors. Those running the business have unlimited liability while the investors have limited liability.

PROS OF LLP

- **A partner is not liable for any wrongful acts of other partners.** Each partner carries their own burden and face consequences of wrongdoings individually.

- **The formation procedure is not long:** When you want to create a limited partnership, it is not tiresome since it only needs approval by the secretary of state.

- **Quick Decision Making:** A limited partnership has a few partners, which makes consultation easier and quicker.

- **There is room for consultation:** Two heads are better than one that is what they say. Partners have a room for discussion before making the final decision. This improves the quality of business decisions made. Partners with limited partnership can leave anytime without dissolving the partnership.

- **Taxation flexibility**

- **Limited liability of the members**

CONS OF LLP

- **They are more expensive to form** than general partnerships.

- **Affected by personal interests:** Most of the times what leads to dissolving partnerships is disagreements between individual partners.

- **Partners with unlimited liability** (those in managerial positions) **suffer** whenever the business cannot pay off its debts.

- **Ongoing state filing requirements**

- **Harder to raise financial capital**

Corporation

This is a business entity owned by a list of shareholders. The shareholders have the mandate to elect a board of directors whose work is to oversee the day to day running of the corporation. When it comes to decision making, it is the responsibility of the directors to make sure that any decision made benefits the corporation and is to support the corporation's objectives. Also, the directors have the power to hire and fire employees. The employees of the corporation have the obligation to make sure that the targets of the business are met within a certain duration of time.

A corporation operates as a separate legal entity from the owners. This means that the owners have limited liability. As a separate legal entity, it means it can buy real estate, sue, and even get sued by creditors. An established corp can raise capital via sale of stock in the stock market. Its ownership can also be transferred from one party to another. It also has perpetual existence meaning that it can continue operating even if the ownership changes.

When you want to start a corporation, most probably you will be the major shareholder with authority to appoint directors. The directors will then hire employees that will be responsible for the running of the company. A corporation operates under corporation by-laws. This is a set of documents that provides guidelines on how the corporation should operate. These by-laws can be modified as the company grows. Every year, the corporation should hold an annual meeting to discuss how the entity has performed.

PROS OF A CORPORATION

- One of the most attractive things about a corporation is that the **owners have limited liability.** This means that in case of debts, the assets of the owners are very safe and remains untouched by the creditors.

CONS OF A CORPORATION

- It is awfully **expensive** compared to setting up simple business setups such as sole proprietorship and partnerships.

- **Starting a corporation involves a lot of paperwork.** For legal paperwork, the owner must file it with the secretary of state.

PROS OF A CORPORATION

- There is a **possibility to lower taxes**, especially when the owner and the business share profits.

- At certain times, they **may deduct benefits as business expenses.**

- **The ownership of a corporation is easily transferable.** This means that in an event whereby the current shareholders and directors foresee a dark future, they might sell the corporation and hence avoid losing their capital investment.

- **Well-structured, organized for better accountability**.

- **A corporation operates as a separate legal entity** and hence is entitled to pay taxes.

- **There is slow decision making** in corporations since the directors must be consulted before it reaches any verdict.

S-Corporation

We base the difference between a S-Corp and a C-Corp on the taxation process. For an S-Corp, there is only one level of taxation. The income generated by the corporation is distributed among the shareholders for taxation purposes.

However, with C-Corps, there is double taxation. The corporation pays corporate tax on its own as a corporation, while the dividends generated by the company and passed down to shareholders are also taxed in terms of personal income tax.

Before you take a step and register your business as an S-Corporation, beware of both the merits and demerits it comes with. The merits include:

PROS OF AN S-CORPORATION

- **Single layer of taxation:** The shareholders of S corporation escape double taxation since the taxes are only payable at the shareholder's level and not at the corporate level. While the business' income continues to be taxable, the shareholders do not carry any extra burden with tax liability.

- **Step up in Basis:** Depending on the amount retained each year by the corporation as income, the shareholders receive a step up on the basis on their stock. This reduces tax liability on the shareholders, especially when the shares are ever sold.

CONS OF AN S-CORPORATION

- **Cash flow vs tax liability:** Whether the shareholders get their share of dividends or not, they are expected to pay their pro rata share of taxes on the company's earnings. This means that a corporation needs to have proper management of cash flow to avoid any inconveniences in this area.

- **Built-in Gains:** When an asset of an S corporation is sold within a 10-year period of S corporation election, then the gain based on the value of the conversion date is taxable to the company. This means that for a corporation which is growing, it is advisable to convert sooner than later to minimize the amount gains within a 10-year period.

Limited Liability Company (LLC)

This is a hybrid of both a corporation and a partnership. A limited liability company operates as a separate legal entity and hence has exclusive rights to buy and own assets, sue or be sued. It has a pass-through taxation feature just like a corporation. This means that the members (shareholders) only suffer from a single taxation, just like in a partnership. Unlike a corporation, it has no stock and involves fewer formalities during the formation process.

The owners of an LLC are called members and not shareholders like in a corporation. This has made many people refer to it as a corporation with fewer complications. This type of company operates under a set guideline of rules referred to as 'operating agreement'. These set of rules can be modified depending on how the business performs over a certain time duration. Operating a limited liability company is less complex since it only requires the members to meet once or twice a year to make or implement certain decisions.

PROS OF LLC

- **Single Taxation**. An LLC does not pay taxes at the company level. The taxes charged are ones that are passed through to the members who later pay personal income tax.

- **Liability protection for members:** The members of an LLC have limited liability, meaning that they cannot take away their assets to cater for business debts.

- They are **easier to establish** compared to corporations since it involves little paperwork.

CONS OF LLC

- They require **more capital to establish** compared to sole proprietorships or partnerships.

- **They require more paperwork and legal procedure.**

Now that you have learned the distinct entities, it is time for you to choose yours:

I choose (business entity)

for the reason(s) of:

*DISCLAIMER: This is <u>not</u> a legal book. I provide the material in this chapter to assist you in understanding basic legal concepts. **Consult with your legal and financial advisors before deciding which structure best suits your needs.**

CHAPTER SIX

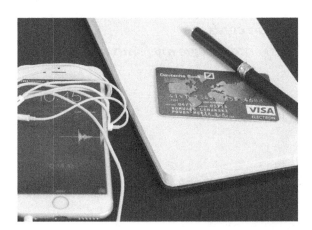

FINANCIAL FRAMEWORK

BUSINESS BANKING

Finding the right bank for your business is very important. Your business banking needs will have different requirements than your personal banking. Whether you are starting a new business or looking for a change from your current bank, it is important that you are not only thinking of now, but the future growth of your business.

When I opened my business, I was referred to my banker/bank by my accountant. She provided me a list of recommendations for banks that she had relationships with. Referrals are always good to have because you know that person has had some type of dealings with that person or business.

I chose my bank because it lined up with my budget at the time, the fees, the knowledge of my banker and how my transactions would be deposited. Before I decided on a financial institution, I met with the banker that had been recommended to me. He asked me a series of questions and vice versa.

The key things that stood out for me were:
- *He asked what he could do for me and listened*
- *He explained online options*
- *I learned about fees for accepting credit cards*
- *I also learned Discover card took longer to receive my funds and some places do not accept Discover*
- *Small banks vs Big banks*
- *Level of experience in your industry*
- *In-person and online needs*

Here is a list of things to look for when looking for a bank:

- How your business accepts and makes payment
- Loans
- Fee structures
- Perks and incentives
- Reputation
- Online Banking

Here are some question to help you along your way.
Keep track of the answers on the sheet to the right.

- ❏ What fees are associated with a business account?
- ❏ What payment options are available through your bank for my business?
- ❏ Does your bank offer online business banking?
- ❏ What are your days and hours of operation?
- ❏ How long does it take for my credit and check transactions to post to my account?
- ❏ Do you offer card processing and how much are your fees?

I recommend you compare 2-3 different banks and go with the right one for you and your business.

BANK #1

BANK #2

BANK #3

CHOOSING THE RIGHT ACCOUNTANT

Q: What is the definition of an Accountant?

A: "Someone who solves a problem you did not know you had in a way you do not understand". -Inc. Magazine

If you are a small business owner and you find yourself starring at the screen, your invoices, accounts payable or your taxes? Then it is an indication that it is time to find someone who is knowledgeable.

First, your specialty is to run your business, your baby! You are passionate about it and you LOVE it! Am I right? So why not have it run like a well-oiled machine behind the scenes too. Let me tell you, I do not know what I would have done without mine from day 1!

WHY YOU NEED AN ACCOUNTANT

Ask yourself to do you really have time to flip through your receipts, figure out which deductions you can count, or which ones do not? Let's face it, your focus and energy are on satisfying your customers and making sure their experience with you is the BEST each time. Definitely not saying to not pay attention to your coins, but let an experienced professional handle the financial load. Business accounting and taxes can overwhelm, so let a professional take care of it the right way. Most time we associate an accountant to just taxes and keeping you abreast on tax laws and changes, but that is not the only services an outstanding accountant can provide. In the beginning I started out as an LLC and as my business grew and changed, I shared my vision with my accountant; she suggested I change it. As I questioned why, she explained the differences between them and I agreed that yes, changing it would be best. Not having an accountant from day one, I do not know if my business would have changed. At the time, I didn't know the difference between the types of business entity. But it is especially important to find the right accountant right for your specific needs and your business.

HOW TO FIND A GOOD ACCOUNTANT

Finding the right accountant is crucial. I found my accountant through a referral from another successful business owner whom I trusted. It may take only one try, but it may take a lot more to find the right fit for you and your business. Everyone's business is unique in their own way. A non-certified accountant may be exactly what you need to handle your business' financial statements, analysis, and bookkeeping. However, with tax advice and return preparation, business owners usually look to accountants who are certified and licensed.

REFERRALS

Ask other business owners about their accountants and their experience with them. Find out who other businesspeople use and how satisfied they are with the services their accountant provides. If you do not or cannot get any worthy referrals using this method, use google or your local phone book (if available) and choose several accounting firms.

When you call, tell the receptionist what you do and ask for the name(s) of accountants familiar with your type of business. Use this information to create a short list of prospective accountants.

Call the 3-5 that you found and ask them about the services they offer.

Ask them about their education (such as whether they are a CPA, Bookkeeper, CMA) and about their experience with your industry. You can also check with their professional association to see if their stated qualifications are valid and there are no outstanding disciplinary issues.

Use this first contact information to choose two or three accountants to interview.

TYPES OF ACCOUNTANTS

CPA-A - A CPA has an undergraduate degree and has met the exam and experience requirements for state certification. A CPA must take continuing education courses to remain certified and licensed.

Bookkeeper - processes the daily record-keeping of all a company's financial transactions. Bookkeepers record the sales, expenses, cash and bank transactions of the business in a general ledger.

CMA-A Certified Management Accountant - CMA is trained to meet the demands of today's accounting requirements besides participating in the company's management team. As with a CPA, a CMA must pass an exam, have business experience, and get continuing education credits.

Take a minute to deliberate on which one is right for you. Answer below:

Now prepare a short list of questions to ask the prospects. My first questions to my accountant were:

1. What can you do for me?

2. Have you dealt with my industry before?

3. Will you be able to deal with my business promptly?

4. Are you fluent with business taxes?

5. How long have you been in business or this field?

Write your own questions below:

KEEPING YOUR BUSINESS SEPARATE

Now that you have your business account set up, you should keep all things business to your business account. Keeping all your business transactions separate from your personal transactions are imperative. Most business entities have regulations that requires financial divisions between the business and the business owner. This was one of the first things my accountant and I talked about when we met and began our business relationship. Again, I was green in so many areas of business.

DUNS CREDIT REPORT

The company to use to establish your business credit is called DUNS & Bradstreet (Data Universal Numbering System). How it works is the system is developed to keep track of businesses around the world by giving them each a nine-digit DUNS numbers. The number is used when businesses seek credit from other businesses.

Things you will need:

1. **Business Entity**
2. **Employer Identification Number (EIN)** (File online or ask your lawyer or accountant)
3. **A stationary address with phone number**
4. **Business bank account**

Once these steps are done you can apply for your DUNS number to begin establishing your business credit without having to use your personal credit for your business needs. This will take some time to establish just like your personal credit, but it does free up your personal without having to use it for both.

Here is an example:

DUNS number 12-3456789

Me: *Hi, my name is Terrance I would like to purchase 100 boxes please and here is my DUNS number 12-3456789.*

Box Company: *Hi Terrance, we have your order as 100 boxes. Is there anything else you need for your order?*

Me: *No, not currently. Thank you.*

Now what will happen, *Box Company* will bill you at the end of the month and just like a credit card bill or car payment, *Box Company* will report to DUNS & Bradstreet your payment history. In turn, if paid on time, your business credit will rise. But if not paid, it will have a negative effect just like with your personal credit. Keeping a great record for your business is great so if you need to get a small business loan to expand your business, re-up on merchandise, products etc. you can do so without any problems and most importantly not using your personal credit to do so.

Box Company

123 Look at me street |New York New York| 555-555-5555

Bill to   Invoice #924501

Terrance Bonner

Amount	Quantity	Description	Unit Price
$125	100	Box pallet	$125

Subtotal $125

Tax 7% $8.75

Total $133.75

COST PER SERVICE

Your cost per service is going to make you or break your business, point blank period! Not knowing this will cause your business to suffer tremendously. I will lay out a few different scenarios to help understand this better. This can be applied to any business structure. When I first started out in my business, I did not know anything about cost per service. I looked around at other places which had the same or similar services as myself, but there is a lot more to it than just looking at someone else's prices.

There are several different things to look at. Not only the service(s) but you also need to include overhead expenses like mortgage or rent, lights, water, internet, scheduling system and paying yourself (which is the main key element) to name a few. You have to factor in EVERYTHING!

COST PER SERVICE = The cost it takes to do the service

LABOR = Your time and energy it takes to do the service

SALE PRICE = What you charge the client or consumer for the service

*****COP** = Cost of Product

*****CPS** = Cost per service

*****CPU** = Cost per Unit

*****USAGE** = How many usages out of product

*****UPS** = Usage per Service

Cost per Unit: Divide COP by Usage = CPU

Multiply CPU x UPS = CPS

This represents your Products:

PRODUCT	COP (COST OF PRODUCT)	USAGE	CPU (COST PER UNIT)	UPS (USE PER SERVICE)	CPU
Massage Lotion	$49.75	75	0.66	1	$0.66
Cake Mix	$1.24	10	0.12	10	$1.20
Cake Icing	$1.50	12	0.13	12	$1.56

	Weekly	Hourly	Per Service		
Facility Cost	$375	$9.38	$2.35	1	$2.35
Labor	$800	$20.00	$5.00	1	$5.00

Source: Angela Green skinbizschool.teachable.com

Use the worksheet below and on the next page to calculate your own costs.

PRODUCT	COP (COST OF PRODUCT)	USAGE	CPU (COST PER UNIT)	UPS (USE PER SERVICE)	CPU

	Weekly	Hourly	Per Service		

PERSONAL/LIABILITY INSURANCE

Acquiring accurate insurance coverage is important for you and your business. Please understand having insurance for your business and personally will save you when and if a time comes when you need it. I remember starting out in business and inquiring about both business and personal insurance. The first one I set up, through a local company, for the business covered equipment, tools, fire, theft, accident if client slips and falls and premises coverage. What it did not cover was me working outside of the business. So, I employ you to discuss and thoroughly cover what your insurance covers and get an understanding of it. One thing I would hate is for something to happen and you think it covers you, and you are not. Ten years in and thankfully nothing has happened, but if something were to occur, I am covered.

Personal short-term disability insurance covers you if something would happen to you if you cannot work. We all want to work as long as we can, but having coverage if something was to happen is always great to have. You would choose the company and what coverage you feel is best for you. I remember starting out with my personal coverage. I was brand new, and was not making a lot of money, so my coverage amount and benefits were low because I was new. That was okay with me because one, it was what I could afford at the time and two, it was better than nothing. Do not feel as if you must get the highest on the list just to have coverage. Stay within your budget and choose what is right for you.

Why do you need it? Liability insurance cover you, your clients and your business in any unexpected event of an injury or accident. Having particular polices in place helps you and your business stay guarded when other try to throw blows at you. Most places it is mandatory to have liability insurance. Not having it is like walking a tightrope for the first time and not having a safety net to catch you each time. Each time we enter a room, we are put at risk. Anything can happen within a session and just what if it does, who or what will help you in that situation? Your liability insurance can and will.

Here are a few things covered for Business Liability Insurance:

Financial Loss: Without insurance, a malpractice or personal injury lawsuit can bankrupt your spa, wellness center, clinic or mobile business.

Asset Loss: If a client sued you, they could take your cash and possibly your car, home and belongings.

Renowned Name Loss: Being the best that you are, word-of-mouth travels fast. Positive news travels slowly, but bad news travels faster than we would like.

Types of Liability Insurance:

Liability Insurance: Only covers an injury for a client. Does not cover you.

General Liability: Protects you from carelessness in result of bodily injury or property damage. It may also cover you if you are held liable for damages to property you rent or lease.

Personal Liability: Provides coverage if any personal injury happens while performing a service on a client.

Business Property Liability: What happens if your business catches on fire? Having liability insurance will cover the damages and loses.

Product Liability: Coverage if any products used to perform services causes any damage or injury during services.

Fire and Water Liability: Covers any damaged or loss of equipment. Be mindful it may or may not cover personal belongings. That may be a separate insurance. Read and understand your coverage.

Damage of Property of Others: This will cover the damage of a client's furniture if damaged during a massage. Perfect for mobile businesses.

First Aid: This helps if you help someone out while medical helps are on its way. Check your policy to see if this is available.

Assault Coverage: If you are assaulted while working. You may be entitled to reimbursement for medical attention.

As you can see, having Liability insurance is great to have just in case something happens. It works if you have it. It will not work if you try to get it after the fact. So start today!

Professional Liability Companies:

American Massage Therapy Association (AMTA)
https://www.amtamassage.org/

Associated Bodywork & Massage Professionals (ABMP)
https://www.abmp.com/

Associated Skin Care Professionals (ASCP)
https://www.ascpskincare.com/refer/769256

Associated Hair Professionals (AHP) including Barbers
https://www.associatedhairprofessionals.com/

Associated Nail Professionals (ANP)
https://www.nailprofessional.com/

CHAPTER SEVEN

BUSINESS MANAGEMENT

BUSINESS MANAGEMENT is essential for a successful business. A business manager is someone who will handle decision making, have exceptional communication skills, leadership skills, motivational skills, problem-solving skills and someone who can delegate. This could be you or someone you hire.

When I began my business, I only had a front desk person. Although it was only one person, it was important for me to learn all aspects of the business from day one.

Although you are the business manager, you often can learn from your employee/s. It is one thing to be alone and do things for yourself, but it all changes when you have to employ someone else to help or do things that are assigned for them to do to help you along your journey.

A vital key to point out is clear and effective communication. As a business owner, you must be able to listen and communicate comfortably with your staff. Listening is a skill that allows your staff to speak out as well and know they will be heard in a non-judgmental setting.

LEADERSHIP is another key component. Having the vision to lead, being courageous, honest and clear focus to lead the way. Leading sometimes can be challenging because of the responsibility of leading others to a goal, to an achievement, to a win or to an accomplishment. It is also extremely rewarding to realize you had your hand in helping someone meet their goal.

It takes a clear and leveled headed individual to help others reach, achieve and aspire to the next level. Going in with motives will not get a leader anywhere but a busted and disgusted team, and no wins for anyone. Let the team recognize you are here to help when needed and to excel.

MOTIVATION is one of my favorite things. Many times, I am motivating others and not knowing it. I love to give out positive energy, so in return I receive it back. I believe whatever you put out, you will receive back. In my outing, on social media or wherever, I like to be that light and positive energy for others because you never know how much you can help someone with just a smile or a friendly gesture.

Inspiring a team whether it is two or one hundred, is a task. For me I do it all the time, but who motivates the motivator? I love educating myself and that is where I get my motivation. Attending, seeing and listening to a topic I am interested in gives me all the motivation I need to continue my journey and to excel in my craft.

Many times, people would say "oh you are always gone or there he goes again". I thrive off meeting like-minded individuals who motivate me to be a better me and in turn help motivate someone else.

"The graveyard is the richest place on earth, because it is here that you will find all the hopes and dreams that were never fulfilled, the books that were never written, the songs that were never sung, the inventions that were never shared, the cures that were never discovered, all because someone was too afraid to take that first step, keep with the problem, or determined to carry out their dream." -Les Brown

LEADERSHIP

Leading with love, positive energy, and a rational mind helps you establish a good relationship with your team and your clients.

Which leadership qualities do you have? (circle all that apply to you)

QUALITIES:

Integrity	*Influence*
Communication	*Empathy*
Self Awareness	*Courage*
Ability to delegate	*Learning agility*
Gratitude	*Respect*

"The quality of a leader is reflected in the standards they set for themselves."

~ Ray Kroc

MOTIVATION

How to get motivated?

For most people, this will be different. I stay motivated by surrounding myself with like-minded individuals with similar goals and interest. If my goal for the next year was to make six or seven figures, then I would find others I connect with to see how to go about doing that. Tuning in to others' journey and downfalls is a splendid start. What works for someone else does not work for the next, but it is a start.

If it is a dream of yours to become a millionaire, you must build your team accordingly. So, to have the best is an understatement. Whatever you do, you want to have the same like-minded people around you. If you cook, you want other bomb cooks around you who see your dream and vision and take it seriously. So much so it motivates them to excel on to hopefully going out on their own to opening their place.

Make a list of the things that motivate you:

THE HIRING PROCESS

Hiring staff can be a nerve-wracking process. However, if you follow these simple tips and steps, you will find the perfect staff members.

Block out time in your calendar so your employees know where you are and how long you'll be unavailable.

Print out the resume of the person to be interviewed. Double check on your calendar to make sure it's the right resume! Highlight anything you wanted to ask them about.

It is natural for a new business owner to be anxious the first time hiring employees. Remember, the interview is just a chance to get to know an applicant. It also provides them an opportunity to learn more about the role and the business. They will be nervous too. I suggest treating them as you would a day spa guest.

CHECKLIST FOR A GOOD INTERVIEW:

❑ What stood out in their cover letter that made you curious?
  What do you feel was missing?

❑ Are there any specifics about the job which may concern you they can't handle?

❑ If your business doesn't have an office space suitable for interviewing, scope out a nearby cafe to have the interview. Make sure it's not too noisy.

❑ Give them a tour of your facility.

Throughout the interview process, it helps to keep in mind that most day spas look for employees who are:

• Attentive to guests' needs
• Professional and friendly
• Comfortable working weekends and evenings
• Flexible

Sample interview questions:

Here are some questions that will help you learn more about the character of your interviewees:

❑ What attracted you to apply for this position?

❑ How would you deal with a troublesome guest?
  Give them a scenario.

❑ What do you do in your role that makes you stand out from other applicants?

❑ It's also nice to ask about hobbies and know them on a personal level.

❑ What continuing education training have you taken that you love the most, and why?

❑ If you knew another staff member was not treating a guest well, what would you do?

Use the space provided to write some of your own questions:

IMPROVING COMMUNICATION

IN THE WORKPLACE

- *Engage employees*
- *Share Knowledge*
- *Focus on problem solving*
- *Encourage original ideas*
- *Facilitate Innovation*
- *Become an active listener*
- *Honesty*

To become what you truly desire, one must strive to be and /or achieve their best along with the best team. To have the best is an understatement, I feel.

Whatever someone does, you want to be around the same like-minded people. They will support and encourage you. If you cook, you want the best meals around. Take what you do seriously. It should motivate you to excel!

I will admit I learned from my mistakes! Value your team! Let them know you believe in them and everyone is in on it together. Even though it's our company, we won't have one if we don't value our team and partners. You can not build a successful business alone.

CHAPTER EIGHT

FORMAL BUSINESS PLAN

For Financial Institutions

There are more than 30 million small businesses in the U.S. which create 1.5 million jobs annually and account for 64 percent of all new jobs created in the U.S., according to the Small Business Administration. In the thought process of starting your business, make sure that you have flexibility to grow. Whether that be financially, self-independence or investing in yourself, the sky is the limit.

Doing your research will help identify your business ideas. With many questions going through your head here are four to ask yourself:

1. *Is there a need for my product|services?*

2. *Who needs it?*

3. *Are there other service providers|companies offering similar products| services?*

4. *How will my business fit into the market?*

Now take a moment to answer those questions below:

Now it is planning time. You will need a plan in order to make your business dream a reality. Your business plan will be your blueprint and will guide your business from the start. By following these step by step guides you will establish yourself as a business and most of all, growth! Without this you will go into business blind and that is not a good feeling or start. It is an important part that you should not skip.

Here is a business plan outline that will walk you through a typical basic plan:

EXECUTIVE SUMMARY

The executive summary is the section that highlights at least one important statement from each of the other sections in your business plan, while also including basic information about your business such as your business name and location, description of your business and its products and/or services, your management team, and the company/s mission statement.

COMPANY DESCRIPTION

The company description section of your business plan is typically the second section, coming after the executive summary. The company description outlines vital details about your company, such as where are you located, how large the company is, what you do, and what you hope to accomplish. This section also describes the vision and direction of the company so potential lenders and partners can develop an accurate impression of who you are.

PRODUCTS AND SERVICES

The products or services section of your business plan should clearly describe what products and/or services you are selling with emphasis on the value you are providing to your customers or clients. This section will also include pricing information, a comparison to similar products or services in the market, and an outline of future offerings.

Here is an example:

MY SERVICES:

Acne Facial, Hyperpigmentation Facial, Combination Skin Facial and Sensitive Skin Facial. Prices $40-$110

Massage Therapy $45-$160

MY PRODUCT

Skin Care including (Cleansers, Facial Masks, Skin treatments, toners, Serums and sunscreen). $40-$150

VALUE (reasoning): The products and services I offer will help my community because 60 million Americans deals with skin acne. I specialize in acne skin facials and treatments. I also offer massage therapy which can help with depression, stress and hypertension to name a few. There are 33% of Americans reported dealing with extreme stress, 77% dealing with stress that affects their physical health and 73% stress impacts their mental health.

Other local competitors in my market are charging $35-$150 for Massage Therapy, Skin care $35-$100.

MARKET ANALYSIS

The market analysis section of your business plan comes after the products and services section and should provide a detailed overview of the industry you intend to sell your product or service in, including statistics to support your claims. This section also includes information about the industry, target market, and competition.

MARKETING STRATEGY

The marketing strategy section of your business plan builds upon the market analysis section. This section outlines where your business fits into the market and how you will price, promote, and sell your products or services.

MANAGEMENT SUMMARY

The management summary section describes how your business is structured, introduces who is involved, outlines external resources, and explains how the business is managed.

FINANCIAL ANALYSIS

The financial analysis section should contain the details for financing your business now, what will be needed for future growth, and an estimation of you operating expenses and gross revenue.

Here is an example:

EQUIPMENT & SUPPLIES:		STAFF		MARKETING
3 Massage Tables	$2,000	Front Desk Associate	Hourly $10 Weekly $400	
10 sets of sheets	$110		Monthly $1600	
Facial 8-1 Machine	$1,500		Yearly $19,200	
Hot Towel Cabinet	$150			
Pack of Towels	$32			
Office phone	$50			
Massage Lotion and Cream	$100			
3 Massage Stools	$100			
Facial Products	$2,500			
TOTAL	**$6,542**			

APPENDICES AND SUPPORTING INFO

The appendix includes information that supports your statements, assumptions, and reasoning used in the other sections of your business plan. This may include graphs, charts, statistics, photos, marketing materials, research, and other relevant data.

If you plan to seek financial support that is the way to go for investors or financial institutions. But if want a simpler route, a simple one-page business plan can give you hope to achieve your goals and steps on how to do it. A plan in writing is better than no plan at all. You can always improve it over time. This quick and easy one-page business plan is great for a freelancing business, basic product or service as a sole-proprietor, LLC, or one-person corporation. A shorter plan will simply fine. Here is a one-page business plan template you can go by:

BUSINESS PLANNING TEMPLATE
SERVICE BUSINESS

BUSINESS PLAN

COMPANY NAME

This section should articulate your hopes and dreams for the business. You can write a vision statement.

For example:

What are you building?

What do you see this business becoming in *x* years?

VISION

How do you plan to grow the business and to what degree? For example, will you hire employees, open branch outlets, or take the business public?

Do you eventually plan to sell the business for profit or to provide money for your retirement?

BUSINESS OVERVIEW (or MISSION)

The business overview or mission should describe how you intend to achieve your vision.

Example of a mission statement:
"To provide Massage Therapy and Esthetic services for therapeutic, healthy skin treatments and relaxation purposes creating the best customer service to individuals, groups and the community. A place where each client is pampered with exceptional customer service. At the Glam Station we adhere to stringent sanitation and disinfection practices to ensure the safety and wellbeing of our clients. These high standards will not be compromised so visit The Glam Station & Spa today." -The Glam Station and Spa

For example:

• What services will you provide?

• What is your target market—who will buy your services?

• How will your service offerings address the needs of customers, for example, what is your unique selling proposition?

• How will you provide your services? Will you offer your services online, through your home business, or at a business location?

PRICING STRATEGY

The pricing strategy section needs to demonstrate how your business will be profitable. Summarize your projected revenue and expenses:

How much will you charge for your services?

Briefly describe how your pricing will be competitive enough to attract customers but be high enough to generate a profit after subtracting expenses.
(Explained in Cost per Service chapter)

Consider a break-even analysis and pricing strategies.

ADVERTISING & PROMOTION *This section describes how you intend to get the word out to customers about your services.*

For example:
What are the most efficient ways to market your services? Will you market them via a business website, email, social media, or newspapers?

Will you use sales promotional methods such as pricing discounts for new customers?

What marketing materials will be used—business cards, flyers, or brochures?

What about referrals?
Referrals are FREE! Referrals come by word of mouth which in turn is FREE. Free is your friend in business because you did not physically have to pay for the business, but you did what was expected which was your best at what you do.

OBJECTIVES Gain five steady customers in the first six months of operation

Earn a net income of $50,000 for the first fiscal year (Fiscal year means a year as reckoned for taxing or accounting purposes.)

List any obstacles or concerns, for example:
Winter season or poor spring weather reduces demand for landscaping services.

ACTION PLANS Briefly describe the action items needed to achieve your objectives, using milestone dates. For example:
By "date" a fully equipped home office will be completed.

By "date" business licenses and insurance acquired.

By "date" launch business website with description of services and price list.

By "date" social media marketing plan in place and potential customers connected via Facebook and LinkedIn.

By "date" subscribed to cloud-based accounting software and setup customer invoice templates.

> One of my favorite apps my accountant and I use for all my receipts is *Receipt Bank*. With this app, all I do is get my receipt, take a picture of it and the app sends it directly to my accountant. The receipt is saved so if I accidentally throw it away or lose it then no worries!

Describe possible solutions for any potential obstacles: *Landscaping services cannot be delivered due to bad weather, investigate providing other services such as snow clearing or tree pruning.*

Keep in mind that a business plan is a living document and you can always start with a one-page plan and enlarge it with additional detail as required.

Questions and Notes:

CHAPTER NINE

RETAIL

Retailing products does not have to make you feel like a salesperson.

- Retailing can be your passive income.
- My strategy for products from day one has been to offer the products that you use in your treatment room.

What better way for your clients to feel the products than to use them on your clients. Whether you are a massage therapist or Esthetician this is the best way to sell to your clients. Why? Because they get to try it before they buy it. What if they have not tried a product? This is the time you educate them on the product and why this will work for them. Be confident in what you offer your clients.

SETTING UP YOUR RETAIL IS VITAL

- Make it visible and close to your check-out
- Have gift certificates available and a sign in view in your rooms. People are drawn to 'signs' and will typically purchase
- Have product information available

- Design an appealing retail section that is easy to browse
- Keep an extra bottle or two of product available so you don't run out. Never disappoint your client
- Keep Inventory. Create a spreadsheet.
    - QuickBooks also keeps track of inventory
    - See your profit margin
- Sample products so people can try
- Train staff efficiently to explain the products. Product knowledge is crucial
- Offer products on your website
    - Online shopping is sky rocketing. (It's how Jeff Bezos of Amazon became a billionaire.)
    - People can be shopping while you are sleeping

PROFIT MARGIN tells you how much the product will sell for above the cost of the products actual price. To determine your profit margin for the product, start with the price you want to sell the item which is what you would charge the client. You would then subtract the cost of the product and how much it cost you, the retailer, to buy it. The numbers you get is your gross profit. Next the gross profit will be divided by what you will sell it for, and that will equal the gross profit margin.

Profit Margin Example:

Your spa offers a variety of products. Today we choose a Vitamin C Serum which you sell for $80. You bought the serum at $40, your mark-up price for each sale is $40. Your margin is a percentage of the selling price. Divide your profit $40 by the selling price which is $80. Your profit margin will be .50 percent. Because 40 divided by $80 is .05 and if you priced all of your prices this way your business would operate at a 50% profit margin on all your products.

UPSELLING A SERVICE

- When upselling you want to concentrate on enhancing the product or service the client is already buying.

- When doing this, you increase profits and supply value to your clients. This strategy is most important.

- While you are learning more about your clients, upselling will come much easier to upgrade their experience by meeting their goals and needs.

- The purpose of upselling is to enhance the possibilities of services and products that may suit their need and increase the complete sale.

- Listening to the client's goals will help you guide them into the purchasing phase they need.

By letting your clients know what you offer, you are building a connection that shows them you are committed to their well-being and to meeting their goals. Sometimes upselling takes a few tries for clients to grasp, but in my experience the more you say it, the more likely the client will eventually try it and enjoy it. The reason I say the client will enjoy it is you have already taken the time to educate them about your offering(s). Perhaps their finances just weren't available the first time you introduced them to the offer. Nevertheless, always offer and educate the client on why it is a great reason to upgrade.

UPSELLING TIPS

- Listen to your clients so you can present the best offer to them, that will meet their needs and goals.

- Always educate your client on the benefits of how and why this upsell is best for them.

- Avoid coming off as a pushy salesperson and just let it flow.

- Follow-up with clients after their appointment to maintain that connection.

UPSELLING EXAMPLES:

1. A client has a massage scheduled but has anxiety. Suggest adding aromatherapy.

2. A client scheduled an eyebrow wax. You notice their lip and chin could also use some attention. Offer to add both to their service as well.

3. A client discloses that she is under a lot of stress and only booked a 30-minute massage. You suggest an upgrade to a 60-minute massage with lavender aromatherapy.

4. A client is buying a skin cleanser. Suggest a moisturizer and sunscreen to compliment each other.

5. A client states he needs to begin scheduling more often. Suggest a year series that includes a percentage off.

Questions and Notes:

CHAPTER TEN

MARKETING AND BRANDING

How to get Published in the News

Who does not want to be published in a national publication or heck on TV for that matter? But how do they know you exist? Where can you go to find these things? I will give you two sources that I use personally. It is so hard sometimes to tell when writers or producers are looking for stories. But the one thing I have learned is to always be ready.

I will be honest, the first few publications I was recognized in, I paid someone to do it for me. There is nothing wrong with doing that, but if you could do it yourself you can save some money. Most times, the publicist or person you're working with has connections which are better than what you would find on your own. They can help with pitching your story or getting you that client, or a particular spot in your chosen magazine or TV segment.

Below is an example of the first publication that was seen on hundreds of news outlets like ABC, NBC, FOX & CBS from 2018:

For Immediate Release
Date
Company Name

Terrance Bonner, the CEO of The Glam Station and Spa wants to introduce his new, trending and beneficial services to the world. Terrance aims to provide the finest Spa Wellness Services to all his customers. The Glam Station and Spa would like to invite everyone to its 3rd anniversary where they will participate in customer appreciation on April 12. 2018 from 5pm-7pm.

Columbus— Date — Terrance Bonner, CEO of The Glam Station and Spa, is heading in the right direction with his company. His company provides a wide range of services like massages, facials, waxing, threading, hair, nails, teeth whitening, lash extensions, and even v-steam. Anything you could possibly want to get done can be serviced at the Glam Station and Spa. Terrance Bonner prides himself on having more knowledge than just massage therapy and esthetics. He constantly raises the bar by not only educating himself on diverse approaches in massage therapy and skin care, but he also educates his clients. The Glam Station and Spa separates themselves from other Spa wellness services by staying ahead of the game. The spa industry will continue to evolve over time, and so will The Glam Station and Spa.

About Terrance Bonner

Terrance Bonner is a native of Columbus Mississippi. His passion is to provide the highest quality in Esthetics and Massage Therapy. In his career, Terrance has obtained a dual license in Massage Therapy and Esthetics. However, his education of Massage Therapy and Esthetics does not stop there. Terrance continues to learn more and more knowledge of his craft as time goes on to develop a diverse approach in giving his massage and skin care clients a unique bodywork, esthetics and educational experience. Not only is he an LMT & LA, but he is also a Mississippi Approved Continuing Education Provider for both the

Massage Therapy and Cosmetology Boards and Licensed Massage Therapy Instructor. Terrance was voted "Among the Best Massage Therapist" 2015, "Best Esthetician" 2016 and "Among the Best Estheticians" 2017. When Terrance is not dedicating his time to The Glam Station and Spa, he is either involved in music—singing and playing the piano or spending time with family and traveling.

Media Contact
Company Name: The Glam Station and Spa
Contact Person: Terrance Bonner, CEO
Address: 1940 Military Road
Contact Number: 662 798 0150
Email-id: Glamstation@yahoo.com
For more information on Product go to website:
  www.theglamstationspa.com

Written with the help of Season Bennett at https://www.socialbarberacademy.com/

This was published for my three-year anniversary of the spa. Even though I paid to get this done, it opened endless opportunities for me and my business. After publication, my business soared, more money came in. I was also requested to speak at different events. This was a totally mind-blowing experience. As I am writing this in the book, two years after it was published, I still get chills thinking how it really propelled my business forward.

You see, getting visible and noticed in a national or even a local publication is exceptionally good for you and your business. It sets you apart and it also most importantly recognizes you as an expert in your field.

Example of a pitch template you can use:

Hi! Editor's Name (use first name if possible),

I am a passionate reader of your publication. I am a Massage Therapist | Esthetician | Instructor whose work has appeared on ABC, NBC, FOX and THE NEW YORK TIMES sites. I have a remarkable story idea(s) that I think would be perfect for (The Outlet) and would really correspond with your audience.

Please let me know if you are interested or would like more information. Thanks so much for consideration - I look forward to hearing from you!

(Your Name & All Contact Info)

P.S I would add or attach here any other publications or press releases.

Take the time to know the market of the publication's audience. Then generate a list of compelling subject lines. You want the subject line to really jump out at the editor. Make it so they will open your email from the subject line alone.

Here are topics that were published:

Glam Station and Spa Wins Best Spa in Mississippi 2019

Massage and Esthetics Authority Terrance Bonner Stresses the Importance of Self-Improvement to Achieve Success

Licensed Massage Therapist and Esthetician Terrance Bonner and His Streak of Achievements in the Wellness Industry

How Terrance Bonner Made His Own Path to Success

Do you see a pattern here? The first two were more so about my business and the last few were about me. Those were establishing me as an expert in my field. The first two brought exposure, but these last few really brought a lot of exposure. So much so, I now had different companies reaching out such as NASNPRO (National Esthetic Spa Network) to write an article, speaking engagements and even to be one of the educators at a virtual Esthetics summit.

Here are two ways you can write your own way to publications and be an expert. One is ***https://www.helpareporter.com/***. There are different payment options to choose from. You do not have to pay for it unless you want to, and of course there are benefits for the paid subscription. The second one is ***Sourcebottle.com***. They are similar, both having paid options. *HelpAReporter* deadlines are usually a 1-3 day turnaround and *Source Bottle* is usually a tad bit longer, closer to a week or so.

Using these two sources alone will get you noticed. Always be prepared and ready to send it out. Especially with *HelpAReporter*. Be on your toes with that one. *HelpAReporter* sends out three emails per day. Each email is different, so you must catch it. Sometimes it may repeat but it is rare. With *Source Bottle* you will receive two emails per day. You can let *Source Bottle* know if you would like to take a break for a week, two weeks or a month and then resume. It can get to be a lot if you're busy, and you may miss some things while trying to meet the deadline of the article at hand. It's worth the time, effort and recognition.

KEYS TO AN AWARD-WINNING BUSINESS

When I began my business, I didn't know much about awards and how they worked. I received my first award a few months after opening my spa. I won *"Among the Best Massage Therapists"* through our local newspaper. I had no idea of this, how one would go about entering, when voting took place, who could vote, or any of it. I will say, it felt good to win and be acknowledged for what I do. In this section I will list key components on how to become aware of what awards are available, accomplish winning them and the opportunities that can follow. Most towns offer this, so you may want to ask your local chamber of commerce what is offered in your area.

KEY 1
Confidence in yourself and your business

First step to all of this is believing in yourself, what you do and have to offer. I doubted myself at times. You have to stay strong and believe in yourself. We all feel unsure of ourselves at times. At the end of the day *you* are your superpower. No one else has that but you!

We sometimes get in our own way. We doubt ourselves because of that one person who has been doing it longer than I have, they have more followers than I do, their clients say great things about their services or products. Okay, so they probably do. You know what is great for them. Now, they are also saying the same thing about you. You are knowledgeable, thorough, great services, products and the list go on and on. So why not you? You are just as great as the next person. You must believe what you are saying and if not, it will convey over as such. Here are three things I want you to say to yourself: I can win, I will win, and I am the BEST.

Writing down your thoughts will help. You may feel like it is a waste of time, but it helps you reaffirm what you want and how you plan on achieving those goals and accomplishments. Write down those goals and its okay to do it as often as you would like. I have found that I reach my goals better once written.

Another fact is sometimes you may have to re-write your goals. Our minds are always going. You may realize your initial goal was too small, that you want to go bigger or vice versa. You may say, let me start smaller. Smaller goals are the realistic, faster goals which can be met sooner, rather than later, giving you momentum to keep going. Writing down your realistic goals is very important. Unrealistic goals waste time, taking away your focus, while letting other things get past you or not accomplished.

KEY 2
Finding the Awards

Once I discovered there was such a thing as receiving business or personal awards, I began doing my research. I began to look at how often certain awards were given. Most often, it was once a year. Next, I researched when an award would begin to circulate for voting. I found out that for the one I had my sights set on, voting began during the summer. Lastly, I researched who could vote, how often, etc. Each entity of award givers will be different, so you want to make sure you read and understand how, when, how many, how much and where you can vote. For one particular business award, the award giver only allowed you to vote via their newspaper. So, you must already be subscriber, or you would have to purchase their paper to vote. As years went on, they incorporated their ballots into both print and online formats.

Now that I have found the award, the next thing to do it apply, apply, apply! You want to let everyone you know to go vote for you. Let your existing clients know because they will be the first to endorse you. They know first-hand how amazing you and your business are. Then, let friends and family know to go vote. In my experience, the less they must do the better. I would have the least number of steps possible. Letting them know what it is, which categories, and a possible link. Straight to the point, so there would be no confusion. I would begin applying locally first, if applicable. Newspapers, Chamber of Commerce, local magazines and TV station. My recommendation is to start here first because you are a local business in the area. People already know of your business and it would be easier for you to place in categories.

Once I got accustomed to how this newspaper award worked, I began looking at other local and state-wide awards. As I stated, I won my first award in 2015 and through the years, I often saw another award being won amongst other local businesses. I had never heard of it (go figure), and didn't know how it worked or even how to apply. This was a state magazine and I wanted to enter. Again, I did not know anything. I had never read the magazine at the time, but I wanted to enter to see how it would go. In 2018, I saw some local businesses had just won their awards with the magazine. I decided to go to their websites to see how one entered their voting process, and when the voting was held. I did my research, found out the award was given in July of 2019, and they would start voting March 1st, 2019. I set a reminder in my calendar for March 1st, 2019 so that I would remember to participate. Yes, that is how dedicated I was to my business being seen and heard. I was not expecting to win. I just wanted to be seen and possibly be one of the top number spas in Mississippi.

March came around and I began the process of entering. I proceeded with my process of telling all of my clients to vote for us in the spa category, and posted it on our social media. I told my family and friends to vote for us. I did nothing out of the ordinary that I haven't done in the past. I sat my team down at the beginning of the process and said, "This is a huge deal. I do not know what I would do if we won this. What I do know is, if we win this, I will take you all wherever it is you would like to go out to eat." I stated that right in our front waiting area. Voting was 2 or 3 weeks long.

In April I got an email stating, "Congratulations, you won Best Spa of Mississippi 2019." I immediately called the rep for my area and asked, "You are saying we won one of the top 4 or 5 right?"

She said "No, you won 1st Place."

I was speechless. I was driving and could hardly contain myself. I wanted to scream on the phone, but I did not want her to hang up on me. I contained myself and hung up very nicely, then screamed as loud as I could. If someone were driving beside me, I am sure they were wondering what was going on. I did not care. I was so excited, surprised and emotional all at one time. We won a state-wide magazine award for *"Best Spa of Mississippi"* She even mentioned how the other reps were surprised as well. She stated, "I told them how determined you were when speaking to you." I was floored that we entered the very first time and won 1st place. This goes back to apply. It does not matter if you have entered once or fifty times, apply anyway. I was confident when I chose to participate. I was determined to win. I knew we were just as good as any other participant in the category. I just wanted my spa name amongst the other great spas of Mississippi.

Now that you have secured local, city-wide, and state-wide awards, you can venture out in national awards. Here are a few to consider:

Green Business Awards - Is your company all about clean and natural products? This award is for you

Minority Owned Award - Are you a minority owned business? Then this award category is for you

Veteran Owned Award - Are you a veteran owned business? Then this award is for you

Women Owned Award - Are you a woman owned business? Then this award is for you

Reminder: Each award process is different, so rules and guidelines may differ from each. Some awards you may have to pay to enter. Just be mindful when entering.

KEY 3
Accepting the Award

Accepting the award is so exhilarating. This will also allow you to have bragging rights. Not in a bad way, but by allowing your current clients and future clients know you are the best. Once you have received your award, or awards, it is time to share with the world and be proud. Depending on where the award comes from, they may have a paid way to say thank you or to publish in their publication. This is one way to say thank you to the voters that do read that publication for voting. I will let you in a little something, shhh, do not tell anyone. But once you have won certain awards opportunities will begin to pour in.

Why? Because you are the best and people want the best! Here are a few different ways you can monetize your winnings.

- Press Release and they are FREE if you do it yourself

- Get published in a magazine. Write an article about your new award and that you are taking care of your community

- Use Catchy headline topics so you stand out. When pitching to an outlet your subject lines should stand out so the editors open your email.

- Get featured in the press or media and send your rating through the roof. Trust me, it helped me when my business was featured on ABC, NBC, FOX, CBS, The New York Times and Kivo Daily to name a few.

Once those things happened and I was able to share those features, the opportunities were endless. I was able to secure paid gigs for teaching, speaking and more clients began seeking me out for my expertise. Now that you are confident in yourself, you can go seek out those awards and monetize your winnings for your award-winning business.

NEWSLETTER

Newsletters keep your customers or followers abreast of what is going on with you and or your company. It should contain news or updates on brand, products or services. Keep your audience engaged and keep a level of communication. Here are tips on creating an effective newsletter:

- Know your clients/customers
- Make your subject line pop
- Visuals are always a good thing to have
- Provide your social media handles
- Provide your contact information
- Always, ALWAYS have a **CALL TO ACTION**

WHAT IS A CALL TO ACTION?

A "call to action," also referred to as CTA, is a term used to tell your clients, followers and potential clients how and what action to take. It can be direct as "Buy Now" or "Subscribe Here". It can be an easy text with a clickable button or link to your services or products.

What could be your Call To Action in your first newsletter?

BUDGET COST OF YOUR NEWSLETTER

A budgeted cost is a projected anticipated expense you and your company will arouse in the future. These are future expectations based on forecasted revenue sales. With budget cost you are predicting what can happen based on growth and client demand.

Example:

My budget for marketing this quarter is $650. The last two quarters we were up 30% so we can increase the budget from $500 to $650 due to sales. I project we increase by 30% more which equals 60%.

NEWSLETTER SOURCES

- Mailchimp
- Constant Contact

What newsletter source will you choose? Research to see which one will best fit your needs.

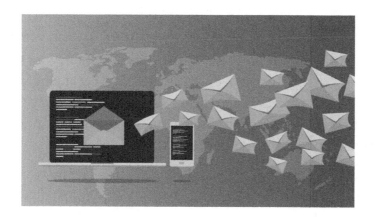

EMAIL LIST

Building an email list is another important piece of your business. Let's say you have all the social platforms there is to have:

- What if one day they all disappeared?

- What would you do? This is why it is great to have a social media presence, but it is always very wise to obtain email addresses as you journey along.

- I've always heard "do not try to reinvent the wheel". That is a wheel that just keeps on spinning.

- Some say emailing is old and outdated. Think about the last time you went to a new website. What was the first thing you saw pop-up? An email box, probably with a gift attached to it, to entice you to give them your email address.

STEP BY STEP BUILDING AND KEEPING YOUR EMAIL LIST

1. Obtain each client email list from your intake forms, website or events
2. Create newsletters to keep engagement with clients
3. Send out coupons, specials or surveys to client
4. Find a system that has automations built in for birthdays, client reminders to come and see you and anniversaries

EMAIL AUTOMATION

Email automation is a great way to create emails to reach your targeted audience without doing the work every single time. By linking your website analytics with email marketing platform, you can target your potential client or customers based on their shopping habits, previous sale and what they prefer. I have used two different platforms.

My first platform was **Constant Contact** in 2014. When I began teaching continuing education class, I needed something that held all the emails I had acquired. By using this, it helped me increase my engagement and improve my results with email marketing automation. This was something that was done once, and it ran itself.

My second system was **Demandforce,** which I used for my spa. This system integrated with my scheduling system *Millennium*. I loved this system because it had everything for my customers.

- **Happy birthday emails**
- **Reminder of visits**
- **Percent off savings**
- **Holiday templates**

My third system was **Kajabi**. This allows me to do more of what I needed to do for classes. Of course, there are plenty of marketing sites out there. You choose the right one for you. I chose Kajabi because it allowed me to

- Host webinar classes all in one place
- Affiliate programs
- Memberships

What email automation system will you use, and why?

Example of how email marketing works:

- **Welcome new contacts** - Automatically send a targeted welcome email when new leads are highly interested in your products or services.

- **Encourage and support your leads** - Create drip campaigns (automated sets of emails that go out based on specific timelines or user actions) to target contacts based on how they interact with you emails.

- **Grow your reach** - Find new clients with sign-up forms.

Here is an example of my welcome email:

> *Greetings (name),*
>
> *I just wanted to take a second to welcome you and thank you for subscribing to my email. I hope something we offer will help you along your journey. If you have any questions or if there is anything else, please reach out to me without hesitation.*
>
> *Thank you, again & Cheers,*
> *Terrance, CEO of The Bonner Institute*

Once you subscribe to my email list you would receive an automated email about me:

Personalize it

> *Meet Terrance*
>
> *Down home Mississippi Guy. Massage Therapist. Esthetician. Entrepreneur. Renaissance Man and founder of The Bonner Institute. Two years ago, I knew I wanted to help other aspiring entrepreneurs and business owners alike. Watching and listening to others as they tried to navigate into business and some seeming to find their way, but most just lost and struggling. The Bonner Institute start brewing. 2020 I made it my mission to help others start their dream the right way. Welcome to the Bonner Institute where your Dreams become your reality.*

Write out what your welcome email might say:

BRANDING

Branding is who you are.

This is different from marketing, which is what you do. To define your brand, first you must define your target audience, your perfect client, and how you want to be perceived. (Complete the exercises on pages 41 and 69 for your target audience and ideal client.)

The definition of brand building is to generate awareness about your business using strategies and campaigns with the goal of creating a unique and lasting image in the marketplace. Positive image + standing out = brand success. Branding can be broken down into three phases: Brand Strategy. Brand Identity. Brand marketing.

Here are four steps to building a successful brand.

1. **Define how you want to be perceived.**
2. **Organize your business based on this promise.**
3. **Communicate your promise.**
4. **Be consistent.**

#1 - PERCEPTION

When I opened my business, the number one thing I wanted my clients to know and see was how clean my spa was. When you walked through the doors, you could see how nice and neat everything was. The bathroom was nice and clean as well. Clients would walk right in, look around and say, "Oh wow! It is so clean in here." Clients like to know your business is clean, especially in times like these. When clients know you stand behind your promise, you will have a client for life. Being organized enough so clients can not only hear what you are saying, but also see it, is of highest importance.

#2 - YOUR PROMISE

What do you guarantee . How will your business represent this promise?

#3 - COMMUNICATION

Communication is key as well. Develop a slogan or a tagline for your business. Our slogan is "Where beauty and wellness are not an option, it's a must".

#4 - ALWAYS BE CONSISTENT

Create a logo that will stand out from the crowd and be bold enough so whenever anyone sees it, they know it is you and what you stand for. Focus on what you want to be known for as well as your personality. Choosing your business is critical to your brand. Does it actually go with what you are offering or promoting? Take my business name, *The Glam Station and Spa*. When I thought of the name, it represented every essence of how and what I wanted my spa to be. I wanted to offer services you couldn't get anywhere else, or that were different from what everyone else was offering. I wanted more of an upscale spa so that I attracted the clientele I was looking for.

- *Tell your story behind your brand, your name and your purpose for opening.*
- *Stay true to yourself no matter what others may say.*

Being a male in a female dominated field was extremely hard. I had to quickly find my niche and set myself apart from everyone else. Because I started with massage first, I was known for massages but after getting my license for esthetics no one really knew what that was. I knew lash extensions and threading were two things that were needed in my area and no one offered it. I set out early in my career of esthetics and invested in myself, after school, to learn those two things. I then was known as the "guy that does lashes and threading". It was all a part of my branding and who I was and wanted my company to be.

Sample Logo created using Canva

BUSINESS CARDS

A business card illustrates your company's brand. Ever heard of leaving an impression? Other than yourself, your business card can speak for you. But you must first have one.

A business card can sometimes make or break a connection. Let your business card convey the particulars like your name, title, email, website, address, and phone number.

What if you left your business card on a table or, better yet, dropped one of your business cards somewhere and a total stranger picked it up?

- *What would their first impression be?*
- *Would it be straight to the point?*
- *Would it confuse the potential client?*
- *Would it be a turn off?*
- *Would it leave a question on what you do?*

Your business card should be very concise. Brand identity your card should reflect the personality of your business which will give the first impression.

Using a distinctive shape also helps your card be memorable. Many companies now offer square, round and non-standard shapes. While more expensive, this is a good way to be unique and stand out from the crowd.

Here is an example of my first business card. This has way too much information. Keep in mind when someone is looking for 'what they need' that must stand out. Your phone number should be easy to read.

> 662.329.9100
> 521 Main Street
> Columbus, Mississippi 39701
>
> **Jon 'Ric**
> INTERNATIONAL
> SALON AND DAY SPAS
> .... THE .... EXPERIENCE
>
> ## Terrance Bonner
> Massage Therapist
> *Monday's by Appointment Only*
> *Tuesday - Friday 9 am - 5 pm | Saturday 9 am - 2 pm*
> • • • • • • •
> *Professional & Ethical Massage*
> *massagebytb@yahoo.com*
> LMT# 1795   Mobile Phone 662.251.9255

Typically, in advertising they will teach your eye goes from the left corner diagonally to the right.

We can use my 1st business card as an example of what NOT to do:

- Massage Therapist should be large so it is seen immediately.
- Phone number should be large and easy to read.
- Hours of operation can go on the back side if you want it.

Notice the difference as I gained more knowledge about creating business cards.

Does the color and image grab attention?

The name of the business stands out more.

My phone number is larger and overall, the whole card is more attractive.

DESIGNING YOUR BUSINESS CARD

When designing your business card try to keep the font simple enough to read your information.

- **Clear and readable Font**
- **Main service or product should be large and seen immediately**
- **Name should be easy to read**
- **Phone number should be large.** People don't want to search or squint to read it
- Color is important if you decide on color. Think of popular business colors and why they use Reds, Yellows etc.
- If you have a logo you can add that as long as it doesn't over take your business card
- Print 500 to start and see if you like them. Are they working for you? If not redesign.
- Do not hold onto your cards. That is not the point. Give 2 or 3 out to everyone!
- Always have cards with you. Never run out.

Use this template as a starting point for your own business card:

BROCHURES

Having a brochure of your menu of services is a great way to advertise yourself and your services. What I have found to be more beneficial is to have just your services and prices on you printed brochures and the descriptions on your website, in which we will get to soon. I found that having the descriptions on your menu takes up a lot of space and makes your menu bulky. If that is how you would like your brochure, please do it however you would like. Here is a sample brochure:

(Front or outside of brochure)

This example is of a brochure called a Tri-Fold Brochure printed in Full Color. This brochure is printed on <u>both</u> sides of the sheet of paper.

There are many options for printing brochures that can make them more cost effective, such as single-sided printing and black and white versus color.

There are also different ways to fold a brochure. You can also choose to have your brochure not be folded.

(Back or inside of brochure)

Use these two pages as a starting point for your own brochure:

TOP

TOP

RACK CARDS

Rack cards are generally 2-sided and are printed on a heavier weight of paper than brochures. They come in many shapes and sizes. Like a brochure, they can be printed in full-color, black and white, or a combination of both. They can be a more economical option than a full brochure, while still representing your business in a professional way. Rack cards work well as handouts for events, too.

SUGGESTION:
- Create several rack cards with symptoms that people can relate to
    - *Ex.* Fibromyalgia: Then add key points of symptoms
    - Add a check list of modalities you may offer to help people
    - You can have one for each of the most popular symptoms you treat.
- On the back you can list
    - Type of service
    - Length of service
    - Cost of service
    - Contact information or website

Use this template as a starting point for your own rack card:

FRONT

BACK

WEBSITE

An online presence is most important now. It allows you to reach your potential client or customer while you sleep. Your website will work for you while you are asleep, on vacation, sick, taking a break etc. Not having one is just not business savvy. You will get your return on investment (ROI) with having your company website up, updated and accurate. This is in addition to your business card. Your business card will lead a potential client or customer to your website to learn even more about you and your company.

With your website, you can explain more about what you offer than with your business card, so embellish here. Talk about yourself, your education and accomplishments. If you have staff, or products, share here in detail. Your website is also where you expand on the details and pricing of the services you offer.

If you sell products you can also list them on a website for sale and increase revenue.

My website recommendations are *Weebly* and *Shopify*.

Popular website companies that will host your website and help you build it are:
- *Wix*
- *GoDaddy*
- *WordPress*

SOCIAL MEDIA

Social Media is here and here to stay. A way to connect with friends, family and way to conduct business. In most instances for free. Being socially present is crucial to your business. Showing clients and potential clients what you are doing is the new norm.

Social media provides a great and unique opportunity and has its advantages for all businesses. Did I mention it was free? A photo or a quick one-minute video can get you clients just like that, in one minute.

Social media includes *Facebook, Instagram, Twitter, Snapchat* and *LinkedIn*. These five are the most popular social media outlets.

- **FACEBOOK** is **social** and people like **interaction**
- **INSTAGRAM** is a **'quick' way to post a meme** of your offerings with contact info
- **TWITTER** is **quick read** and great for last minute specials
- **LINKEDIN** reaches more **professionals**
- **SNAPCHAT** is **fun**

Ask yourself where is your *'ideal client'* hanging out.

Some benefits to using Social Media:

- Client Interaction
- Increased traffic to your business
- More Sales
- Little to no expense
- A more national reach

Facebook Example:

- Set up a fan page for your business
- Keep it <u>professional</u>
- Educate your ideal client
- Do short videos to create a relationship
- Post specials
- Post inspiration – people love that
- Ask engaging questions

Your personal page on social media should be professional as well, although you engage more personal vs business.

CHAPTER ELEVEN

OPENING YOUR BUSINESS

You've done all of the planning, identified your target audience and your ideal client, written your business plan, secured your funding, designed your brand and created your marketing materials. Now it's time to open you business!

PRESS RELEASE

Why a press release? A press release can solidify you from the rest. Once you have released your press release, you can use it as leverage for your company on social media platforms, as well your website for future and potential clients to see. It is something you can do yourself and it is no cost to you.

WHEN TO RELEASE

Here is a templete for a press release for your business

Sample Press Release:

FOR IMMEDIATE RELEASE

Contact Information

(Company Name)
(Contact Name)
(Phone Number)
(Email Address)

(Company) Announces the Launch of *(state the information you need to share) Include your* **WHEN, WHY and WHERE**

(City, State)-(Company) is excited to announce the launch of *(product|publication|campaign),* a *(description of product|publication| campaign)*

(CALL TO ACTION)

For more information, please contact *(Owner)* at *(phone number, email)* or visit their website at *(www.website.com)*

ADVERTISING

The phrase *"it takes money to make money"* is true. It costs to make business cards or develop a website.

What does advertising offer you and your clients?

- Be consistent with ads
- Keep your name and what you offer in front of future clients
- Keep content fresh, enticing and relevant

If you get no response, you may not be reaching your clients needs. **Know your ideal client.**

LOCAL TV STATION

- I set a budget of $300/month for 15 seconds. It was my best ROI (Return On Investment)

- 30 seconds was $500 and gave me more time to be very clear on what I wanted to convey

MAGAZINES

Check with your local magazines
- Wellness magazines or journals that reach your target market

Choose the budget that works for you.
- Business card side
- 1/8 page, 1/4 page or more

National Magazines – will that reach your target audience?
- See if they are seeking articles
- If you sell products online, this may be a viable source to expand your business.

LOCAL NEWSPAPER

- Write articles pertinent to the needs of your community
- These don't cost anything
- Place an ad with a coupon for first visit
- Find out how many people read the newspaper, who their main market is, and if it targets your ideal client.

RADIO SHOWS OR PODCASTS

- Podcasts are very popular and typically hosts will interview you for free or a nominal costs
- Radio shows pertaining to your service look for people to interview as well. Research what is available in your region.

GRAND OPENING

Congratulations! Your big day is here! Let's prepare you for a successful opening with the following checklist.

CHECKLIST

____ Did you sent in your press release and/or write an article about your Grand Opening In a community newspaper?

____ Do you have all the required marketing materials available for your new clients?

____ Is your social media page set up and have you been pre-promoting with videos, special offerings and educating your followers?

____ Set a Grand Opening Date

____ Make sure all staff you may have is available

____ Announce it in newsletters, social media and community calendars

____ Decide what 'gift' you may hand out to customers

      A goodie bag
      A voucher for a discount
      A sample of product

____ Will you have snacks available for your customers? People enjoy simple snacks and drinks. It makes them feel welcomed.

____ Will you offer a sampling of your service or product

      Chair Massage
      Short lectures to educate
      Free stuff

____ What are the hours of your grand opening

____ Did you tell local supporters and businesses

____ Schedule a ribbon cutting ceremony with the Chamber of Commerce and local representatives

____ Invite local newspaper reporter

PRE-OPENING/PACKAGES

A spa, wellness center or clinic is available well before you open your doors.

- Make money before your doors open
- The world wide web is flourishing with social media apps and it is almost unheard of to keep news about opening out of the public's hand

HERE ARE A FEW WAYS TO CREATE A BUZZ:

GRAND OPENING CONTEST

COUNTDOWN – post on social media, send a newsletter. Offer a coupon of freebie when they show up for the Grand Opening.

TEAM INTRODUCTIONS (if you are solo do a whole promo about yourself. Do not be shy)

SPECIAL OFFERS/PACKAGES

- Pre promote these packages.
- Purchase prior to the Grand Opening Date
- Make it irresistible
- A pre package offering should have a large enough discount that people will want to jump on it
- Don't be afraid to offer BOGO. Buy 1 Get 1 – It's cheaper than ads and gets new clients in your door

OPENING DAY OFFERS

Examples:

3 - 1-hour Massage Series	**$195**	*Save $30*
6 - 1-hour Massage Series	**$410**	*Save $40*
3 - Facial Treatment Series	**$225**	*Save $30*
6 - Facial Treatment Series	**$470**	*Save $40*

Create your list of Grand Opening Ideas:

Design your own pre-opening promotion idea:

CONCLUSION

I hope you found this information valuable to get you started.

Remember the following three tips every business needs to succeed.

1.   Choosing the Right Business for You

We all have ideas, but is that one the right fit for you? Business can be extremely rewarding if done and planned correctly. Start by writing down several choices, then choosing your top 3-5. From there do a test run. Try it out before you take that final leap. By doing this you will see who likes it, who does not and the possibilities that can come from it. Besides, making the right decision early will only help in the long run.

2.   Be Uniquely Different

What do I mean you ask? What will make you different from your competitors? Now, I am not saying you must compete with them by any means, but what will differentiate you from them? Finding your niche that will set you apart from the rest. Finding that targeted audience, your customer service, the way you market your business. I will take all the above for 100% please! Be uniquely you!

3. Staying Dedicated

Starting a business may seem easy, but staying dedicated and committed is the hardest part. There will be ups and downs, but in business, you must keep going. Repeat after me, "Whatever it takes, whatever it takes, WHATEVER IT TAKES!!" Remember my core value? DETERMINATION!

That is what will get you through anything. You will get tired; you will not want to show up. But just think back to why you began. All the sacrifices you made to even start. Therefore, it is important to think a lot about that first step. Beginning right will lead you to more success than you could ever imagine. Take it from me, I did it and so can you!

If you have questions or would like to attend a workshop please contact me.

www.TheBonnerInstitute.com
BonnerInfo@yahoo.com

ABOUT THE AUTHOR

Terrance Bonner is a native of Columbus, Mississippi. His passion is to provide the highest quality service in Esthetics and Massage Therapy. In his career, Terrance has obtained a dual license in Massage Therapy and Esthetics. However, his education of Massage Therapy and Esthetics does not stop there. Terrance continues to learn more and more knowledge of his craft as time goes on to develop a diverse approach in giving his massage and skin care clients a unique bodywork, esthetics and educational experience.

Not only is he an LMT & LA, but he is also a Mississippi Approved Continuing Education Provider for both the Massage Therapy and Cosmetology Boards and a Licensed Massage Therapy Instructor.

Terrance was voted *"Among the Best Massage Therapists"* in 2015, *"Best Esthetician"* 2016 and *"Among the Best Estheticians"* 2017. When Terrance is not dedicating his time to his business, *The Glam Station and Spa*, he is either involved in music—singing and playing the piano, or spending time with his family and traveling.

www.PPP-Publishing.com

Made in the USA
Coppell, TX
30 April 2022

77264516R00098